Nevertheless, *hello*

ALSO BY CHRISTOPHER GOODRICH

By Reaching

Nevertheless, *hello*

CHRISTOPHER GOODRICH

STEEL TOE BOOKS

BOWLING GREEN, KENTUCKY

ISBN 978-0-9743264-9-8

STEEL TOE BOOKS
Western Kentucky University
Department of English
1906 College Heights Blvd. #11086
Bowling Green, KY 42101-1086
steeltoebooks.com

COVER PHOTO
"Dance" by Kara Thurmond and Andrew Amelinckx, 2008
karathurmond.com

COVER AND BOOK DESIGN
Molly McCaffrey

For my parents, every last one of them.

And for Rachel.

CONTENTS

CHAPTER ONE

Men are from Earth, Women are from Earth

I'll admit, the idea of a woman
traveling from Venus to love me
is flattering, but ultimately
ridiculous. I'll admit,
love requires some inattention
to truth, but if we are to get anywhere
as a people, as a nation,
if we are to be taken
seriously, we must know the limits
of lying. I, for example, live in New York,
a city so devoid of space
it's unbearable.
I'm not the first to come home
to a modest street in Brooklyn
and look to the stars,
or to be more accurate, star.
I am not the last to touch a woman
whose grace I mistake
for moonlight. And if she and I
are outside one ripe evening
gazing upward simultaneously,
some dear October
when all the star are out,
we are not looking for relatives—
we are asking for courage, guidance,
a witness. Dear universe, riddle
of light and love, my name is Chris.
This is Rachel. Remind us of the facts.
We want to start this thing out right.

Love Letter to a Woman Who Refuses to Recognize my Existence

You step into my life
like most people step onto a train.

By lifting your right foot, then your left.
Wondering where to store your luggage,

looking for a seat next to someone
who will let you read your Tolstoy

in peace. Who wants to talk
about how they are living, what they do

for money? Not you. Not me.
We are here to ignore each other.

We smile while we do so,
pay attention to pastured cows.

We are getting somewhere
without speaking. You are not

up to being entertained,
I am not interested in faking sincerity.

And my life is on the verge of disappearing.
I'm bored with everything I can't touch.

I open my mouth because you are stunning
against the glass, the green, the blue, wet white

and gray. How are you living, I say,
What do you do for money?

I'll call you my Isabelle.
I haven't spoken for days,

so, I'll start the conversation.
Let's talk about some people,

and why they choose to read alone.
Or how we will survive a long-distance relationship.

What about Charley if it's a boy?
How about Gregory if we make him a brother?

To the Woman Whose Nose Ran into Our Frisbee, July 13th 2003, Ft. Green Park, and To the Blood that Would Not Stop Gushing

You have to understand. We have never done this before.
Together, I mean, and in public.
We are still adjusting to passersby. You, for example.
We are learning the weight of wind.
Deciphering speed. Calculating distance, aim.
The sun is a factor. Shadow too. And season.
If it were Spring, say, my mind would focus.
So discontent I am during long winters,
when I finally step on new grass
all I think about is how to get a disc
through my fingers and into someone else's.
But this is summer.
There are bells going off every four seconds.
Everyone is eating ice cream.
Dogs are running without leashes.
Sometimes women tan themselves without bikini tops
and I begin dreaming my old dreams again.
And laugh as I do without thinking.

This is not the first time
you've been hit in the nose,
I'm sure, so full it is of itself.
But I have never seen someone drop to the ground
the way you did. First to your knees,
and then with your forehead hitting the dirt
as if you were worshiping us.
The blood a kind of myrrh. Myself a wise man.

The Frisbee a flying baby Jesus,
tossed to teach us sin, atonement, knowledge, sorrow.

Your nose is a little crooked now.
And believe me, somewhere I am dying a little
thinking of you. Hiding in the chaos of knowledge.
Somewhere I am always releasing a Frisbee,
reliving that moment—not the one of brutal contact,
the moment two seconds before, once it has left my hand,
seeing you smile at me for the last time.

First

Because I wasn't in love with the girl
I wasn't planning on doing it,
I wasn't comfortable being that guy,
though surely, once into breasts
and skin and tongues thrashing
like caught fish, love wasn't a problem.
I was inside of her—I don't remember how—
my shirt clinging to my chest,
my socks tight around my calves—
no blank verse, no talk of patioed
suburban futures—part rented movie,
part flank steak—but my pants were around my ankles,
I remember that clearly—navy blue corduroys
positioned there, I'm guessing
because my shoes—brown, stripped
Rockport casuals—hadn't yet been untied.

We dated for six months after that,
another six sweaty months of me
doing that awkward thing in my clothes
because I didn't know how, because
I hated my body, because I was a lie
of composure in love with Melissa.
Jenny, I called her that very night,
which you knew, you knew, you knew I think,
and if you are listening, which some part of me
must believe, tell me if this is the same ache
that wakes you before the alarm,
an ache that lights the book of our remembering.

It was my loneliness learning the world.

October

Your father snores
downstairs with the television on.
He doesn't know I'm here, cleaning
your room—the air stale,
and old habits in need of mothering.

Your bed is made. Dust, dusted.
Everything in order.
But the old pictures—
I don't know, something
in the light there,
the way our smiles scatter
around each other.

I think we loved you
a little less than your brother.
I'm sure of it.

It's quiet now. The pinched
moon rotates the night.
It's not until I watch
the ground collect what falls
that I recognize you:

your arms folded, the room vacant,
but for me, who'd like to call this emptiness her own.

BECAUSE IT'S IMPORTANT

I will wake up early tomorrow
and because it's cold, I will put myself on carefully
and I will run the warm water before rubbing my hands together.
I will look for my keys, which will have wandered,

and I will kiss you and cover you and tiptoe downstairs
into the empty spaces of last night's conversation,
over the rickety spine of our new marriage,
past the ghosts of our still-damp screaming,

round to the car that will take me to my crestfallen mother.
She will likely be cleaning something upon my arrival
and I will stand in the doorway
looking for the woman who won't be expecting me,

the one who drove me to Dad's on her weekends.
I hope to sparkle for her in the light.
I hope to offer every kindness
and I expect we'll share a cup of something hot

to melt our tongues of old miseries.
She will want to know how the drive was
and I will begin with the only words I have:
How are you doing? And how have you been?

You, Me, My Mom, My Dad

I'm told I'm looking for mother and father combined,
which means you will be bald and co-dependent.

I will blame you for their shortcomings, applaud
you for their success (a thing you will measure

by how often the children come home). Praise
the rice pudding you'll know how to make,

and god love you for the $50 on my birthday
with notes that read Dearest Christopher,

We love you over and over, Mom and Dad.
I make love to the half that brought surprise snicker bars

home when I was four. And afterwards,
I hold the half that tucked me in at night,

the half that made me a sister. In your four eyes,
I am already reliving myself even as I try living

up to you, which is absurd. You hold my car keys in your hand,
scold me for coming in past curfew, out with an older girl.

I know I should have called. I apologize for not doing so.
Tomorrow, let me stay home with the kids so the two of you

can see a movie or dine finally alone. You don't have to
                                                    like her,
but I will tell you this: her name is Rachel. I'm going to
                                                    marry her

as many times as I can.

ICARUS EXPLAINS

I was born a very young man
with a face, as mother said, for sky,
not knowing which past was mine,
what course could hold me.

My father, a man of silent sadness,
troubled by the wood and wax
of science, had nothing to do
with my counting to ten,

learning the bicycle.
I was the convenient hello
between projects, someone
he'd pass in the kitchen

and swear was his son.
Over time, not knowing how
to throw a ball, swing a hammer,
I became the small bird

fallen asleep under his arm
and one summer, seventeen,
lost in a maze of misunderstanding,
I vowed to fly on my own.

Sometimes my bones
were so heavy they begged a father's voice
to call from the next room.
I remember his workshop,

saying goodbye. I remember the touch
of his grizzled hand stopping me.
I remember feathers. In the end,
I don't know what I wanted.

His eyes were on me. His hands
fastened the great work to my shoulders.
He wanted to see what I could do.

Poem in my Head All Morning

Of all the people living inside of you,
and all the people living inside of me,
surely we can find a suitable pair

willing to go for coffee,
willing to do what others
have talked about for years now.

CHAPTER TWO

Extraordinary Sex Now!

Sounds simple enough.
You lie down with your legs apart
and I lie on top of you
thinking of snow or field
or Rumi.
You with hints of horizon
position yourself to see
the night clearly. I take
your hands—lifeboats.
Press them to my eyes,
place my penis
on your round belly,
drag it down the gardens
and pathways
of your complicated auroras.
I listen to your gentle jingle,
the small sounds
you make when you think
you are making none at all.
The book I'm reading
tells me to take my time.
I can't rush past the breathing
and heartstuff.
We need to hold hands,
we need to expose our hidden rituals,
we should shit in front of each other.
Eventually, we will begin speaking again.
Slowly at first, in moans,
and then two or three

sentences at a time
with words like begonia and supper in them
until our movements are as natural
as sun or wind or depression.
Until I become spontaneous
and impolite, ask you
to open your legs,
your eyes,
that I may look at them.
I have it all figured out.
The room empty but for a single polyester pillow,
the lighting like a second chance,
grapefruit, pineapple singing in the corners,
a slip of red silk hanging center
in the shape of a violin.
A small velvet box.
A ring inside.
It's bound to work.
Bound to.

* *Extraordinary Sex Now* is the title of a book by Dr. Sandra
  R. Scantling, published by Doubleday, New York, 1998.

SAY IT WITH A MIX-TAPE

These are the professionals. The ones who know
why birds suddenly appear every time you are near,

the self-assured idols who can ask *Do you
want to know a secret ooooo waaaa oooooo?*

without sounding stupid. I've begged
them to explain why secrets are

given as gifts in obvious packaging.
So much of falling is sitting still, filling

a blank tape with voices of the famous—
the mystic warbling of Joni Mitchell,

the simple sex of Simon and Garfunkel.
This is what it sounds like to be me in love with you.

And because only Ray Charles, who sings from both sides now,
can read my heart's handwriting, I've included

two of his numbers, see side A, songs two and nine.
He will insist, as many times as you care to listen:

*I'm gonna love you like nobody's loved you come rain
or come shine,* which, incidentally, is true, I'm gonna.

The Mix Tape: proof that love loves James Brown, the reason
we turn to Nina Simone when sex fails to fulfill us,

why, when harmony is what is missing,
a light rhythmic rain begins to fall.

TOOTH FAIRY DIES

No explanation.
Just the bloody molar
ziplocked tight,
right where I left it
late last night.
How easy to convince myself
of her death,
crushed by the unexpected
weight of additional gold—
a result, I know, of pulling
before it was time.
I can even,
if I allow it,
hear the thud
of something pure
hitting the closed window,
falling three flights.
Time to explain
myself to mother.
Someone has to tell
the other children.
But she, seeing my lowered head,
my outstretched hand
holding that little piece of me
I was willing to give
for the right price,
gasps aloud,
rushes to her purse
and before I open my mouth,

hands me two dollars,
apologizes profusely.
We both know what has passed.
No need now to discuss it.
Everything is changing.
The world is becoming
a dangerous place.

Josh Roberts, Suicide

Hours from now you jump
from a Brooklyn rooftop. I return
haphazard-like, to pick up an umbrella
and hear the news from a friend.
I sit down. I have to.
Then crawl four flights
to the strict city street for work at 10am.

For now, it is morning.
The two of us sit in Brooklyn's
botanic gardens. The sky is a summer
sheen. Your talk is a thousand stories
and a hundred people you haven't touched.
You cannot get away from caring.
And receiving is another matter,
another gift.

I'd like to help you, but I can't.
I can't. What I can do
is tell jokes. I'm good at jokes.
I would call it precious, this sitting.
But precious is the wrong word now
when anger, finally, is all
I have. Not sadness. Not yet.

Once you are over, Josh,
the birds will not leave their singing.
Impossible. The rain will not stop
its falling. Only you will stop.

And the rest of us will do the things
we love, the things that move us
towards doing. The wretched and regal
and right things that make this world
so desperately true.

As Brothers

In addition to death,
we practiced, as brothers, leaving
until one evening, the rain
fingerprinting our windows,
we hit the cool of a loneliness
I could not ignore.

Have you ever traced a silent war
across the length of your life?
Have you known an enemy
so frank with shattered music
you began to love him on the sidewalk
in front of your house, searching the sky
as brothers, until it's impossible,
your eyes granite, your voice
a forged and faded signature, until one of you,
not knowing what else,
presses the gas and drives away?

I must have waited for hours
on that curb, I even thought
to shout your name, I needed to
explain something fleeting,
dotted with both of our failures.
But I never did. I returned home
to make roast beef, creamed corn
with my beloved and for that too I apologize.

You and I could have made dinner
together, talked about tomorrow
the way friends do, made the ice tea, sweet and cool,
we both love, and you could have handed me a napkin,
and I could have passed you the butter.

Our Elephant

So thin was he on arrival I knew
he was not long for this world.
But after hours, he found
the kitchen pantry, shoveled in
shovelfuls. After days he found
the weight set, knew which routine
worked when. Gorged himself
on carbs and protein. Cried for love,
affection, suits by Armani. After weeks,
he groomed himself gorgeous, cut nails, cleaned ears.
After our memories, fears,
he devoured the classics: Nietzsche,
Swift, Dickinson. Practiced
Catholicism, Judaism, Fascism,
and since he was not working days,
opened our mail, pissed on our walls.
There was no end to him.
In that first month, he gained 4000 pounds,
the first 3500, pure muscle, adrenaline.
He lectured on emotional poverty, suicidal
indifference. I woke to cold showers,
the curtains on fire. I should have suggested
counseling. Someone should have said something.

Years later,
a staggering 17 tons, we couldn't leave the apartment.
We couldn't find the door. Our elephant
became roof, lawn, table, tile. He required blood, tears,
mucus, bile. Then pointed to our bones.
Which we gave, without question.

What the Night Brings, What the Morning

When she appeared, suddenly,
pushing his bedroom door open

like she meant it, stepping off
the midnight moon like a sweet

tongued hallelujah, he slid to the lumpy side
without thinking, so that after a night

of claiming themselves, she would sleep
comfortably on the side that boasted

all its springs, and he would be first
to the shower, the way he liked it,

howling "Amazing Grace"
as if it were his, filling the tiled corners

with How Sweet the Sound. And she,
who would wake up sometime later,

would paint Les Demoiselles d'Avignon
as if it were the thing to do before breakfast,

as if this were the time to better
whatever Picasso got wrong.

By Reaching

The first time I climbed a woman
her belly filled with tears,
a kind of wet loathing,
and I touched her skin
for I knew loathing myself,
but about tears I had to be taught.
We slept on our backs then
our sides now,
and if I still run from things too difficult,
at least, lately, I'm leaning differently,
leaning as a way of reaching,
asking as a way of answering her questions,
loving her one phone call at a time,
with what I hope is decency,
my sleeves rolled up,
my palms facing out.

OUR RELATIONSHIP TURNS 7 MONTHS OLD

It is teething
and sitting up.
Making the most

peculiar sounds
and drooling, oh god,
is it drooling.

Three months
and it will discover
its feet. Falling down

and up, bouncing,
twirling. For now
it is crawling,

though we don't
call it crawling.
We call it

something sounding
like "mama,"
but really

we are just putting
our lips together,
talking them apart.

We put everything
into our mouths,
dependent, as we are

on this little world.
It revolves around us.
Look, look at it spin.

CHAPTER THREE

ART OF LEAVING

I'm thinking of approaching
the woman with the blue cut-offs,
the sad hair and eyes, the one
lying in the grass on her back,
her knees together, a bit of cloud
on her belly. I'm thinking of strolling
over, looking absently at my feet
before focusing, before saying,
I will love you for the rest of my life,
before saying, I have never loved anyone
in the past five minutes
the way I have loved you,
I've named our three children,
I'm saving for their education,
I'm ready to accept you as you are,
the fact that you hate to read,
the fact that you are no longer speaking
to your father, I will hand you my heart,
I will lob it gently in your direction.

But should there be pain in our future,
freezing arms and burning lungs,
if there is naked jealousy
and stunted prayers,
if we must live and die with tortured stomachs,
cry about money and friendship,
failed identity and half lives,
you should leave now. Forget what I have said.
Forget that I was made to love

your tiny knees, your fruitless theories.

And she will leave. Without speaking.
First rising, her arms fold across her chest,
she retrieves the blue blanket
that has kept her from the dirt,
and removes herself from my trembling
sight forever. She will turn back once,
a strange smile curling her lips,
before reaching the dirt road,
the one that will carry her home,
her sandals clapping her heels
with each precious step.

Because failure is sweetest
when discovered in loved ones,
I spent years discovering you,
a decade on someone else's shoulder
before lifting your ghost
to my back and carrying on. How
many summers playing football
baseball, football, then soccer,
watching the goofball movies
of our friendship fart away?
The heroes we must have dreamed of,
the promises we nearly became. Then
suddenly, the train that carried you away,
whistled twice and left.
                                        I stood
on the platform, counting rails.
Blaming those who stepped off
for what I became without you,
armor and debt. I suppose
I've continued counting
though I'll never admit it,
you bastard. After nine years
I'm still pretending
you have nothing to do
with who I choose to love.
                                Amazing
how we survived each other. Almost
beautiful my ability to recognize failure
and call it survival.

This Poem Will Not Save Your Life

After seeing a book titled THIS BOOK WILL SAVE YOUR LIFE

Nor will it walk the dog, forgive
your debt, fetishize your feet.
It will not weep for your children,
beg you to stay, pull the possible
world over your heart like a sunrise.
This poem will not blame your husband,
threaten your wife, help you to fail.
This poem will not lie to your face,
judge you for who you aim to love.
What it will do is take up space,
collect dust, yellow with time. What it will do
is exist. As complicated and necessary
and frightening as that. As futile.
But it will not save your life. You
have to do that yourself. And you can.
Listen hard. Look into my eyes:
Someone is calling your name.

As the Train Pulled into the Station

Before she gathered her two belongings
and ambled toward the open doors,
we sat across from one another
the way people do when they don't know what they're
                                              looking for
and I tried to time it so that, as she looked away,
I could look at her without her noticing,
but I must have forgotten who I was,
what the goal was, what the game,
because twice I failed
and twice her suspecting gaze
caught my eager own and held it
for as long as one thing can hold another
without killing it. For as long as that.

Before standing, turning, disappearing,
she paused for what must have been dust to this world,
and turned her head slightly to the right
to see whether or not I was still playing,
she nearly made my departure possible by doing so,
and if I had known who I was I would have followed,
I would have asked for her name, her theory on adultery,
But I did not. As awkward as it was, I returned to the woman
who cheated on me two weeks before.
And after sitting for a long time on a curb
across the street from our apartment,
I stepped quietly through the door
so as not to wake her,

it was very late besides,
and once under the covers,
I told her I loved her, in fact, I can't explain it,
we made ferocious love, and certain as regret leads to regret,
while reaching orgasm she stopped,
just like that she stopped
and asked who I was thinking about
and I told her, without looking at her, I told her
I'm thinking about you and she paused,
saying nothing, saying nothing,
and I said, without seeing her this time,
without even knowing if she was in the room, I said
All I'm thinking about is you.

First to Wake

If you are first to wake,
do me a favor and turn off the alarm,
let the dog out to pee.

I would, but I'm far away now,
standing on a bridge that hovers
above a living riverbed,

speaking Latin to someone
who speaks it back. I am turning the pages
of guilty pleasure, strolling the gardens

of invincible men, kissing as many girls
as I can before interrupted by traffic.
If you are still looking for something to do

after watering the lawn,
there are breakfast sausages in the fridge,
they need cooking or they'll turn on us.

You could prepare them with eggs or oatmeal,
thinking all the while of the conversation we'll have
as I make my way from the bedroom,

our comforter wrapped around my shoulders,
my stomach rumbling from the emptiness
of waking up alone. And if you haven't already

left me for someone who wakes with you,
if you haven't run off with one of the street men
who keep their eyes on you,

you might take a moment to turn the radio on,
something classical, or in any case,
something to soothe me back to sleep

in the event I am startled awake
by the clanging of pots, the slamming of doors.

Drinking Together, Li Po and I Admire Wang's Garden

We go back and forth like this:
Raising our gin-soaked chins
to a translucent daytime moon,
toasting the indecent goldenrod,
the sweet sting of morning,
memorizing the hibiscus
then falling deep into an unbelievable 10am.

Last night, a dozen friends joked
as you stripped clean and rode the rope
swing into the river. Afterwards, the wine wet,
the grass low and dying, we vowed to cherish
the balding crocus in sickness and in health.

This morning we watch the birds
return one by one to Wang's roof,
our backs against the same oak,
our tumblers now empty.
I am drifting in and out of consciousness
but you are still awake, writing something down,
transfixed by willow-blossom, the call of the moon,
willow-blossom, moon, blossom, moon.

GOING TO BED ANGRY

We know so much about struggle,
and putting our clothes away,
so much about this hard-wood house
and its dust, but nothing about penguins.

Yes we waddle, but not the way
one waddles toward something warm.
Not the way one waddles
in the frigid sun of a midnight

arctic to find a wife,
the way a penguin does
once a year, returning,
returning to love.

Tonight, we are going to bed angry.
Too many terrible things need saying
but now is not the time.
Let us lie with anger

until it knows the way we walk
out of a room, the way
we look into mirrors
practicing our speech,

the way, finally, we return
to bed with nothing or with fists—
their impossible opening and closing.
It is how we hold on to everything,

how we knock on the door
of our making, asking, begging
sometimes, to be let in.

If I Didn't Open My Arms

I'd be lying if I said you meant everything.
I'd be lying if I didn't open my arms.
This fire is true and the rest,
I mean everything, somehow also true.
The way a river drowns what it loves.
That's how much I love you.

Chapter Four

SPOTLESS

After fire forced our friend
to the ledge of the eighty-fourth floor, I started small:
alphabetized poetry, separated pens
from pens, black from blue.
Scrubbed two toilets, a moldy
bedroom ceiling, perfumed stale air
with hickory, dusted both televisions,
watered a dying kitchen cactus, vacuumed
the living room carpet. Nothing is sweeter
than sparkling porcelain, scrubbed dishes,
bleached sinks. I picked hair from every drain
I remembered, killed the bacteria mating in my mouth.
Four loads of laundry later, I polished my image
into the stovetop. And how the roaches suffered!
I singled out each lone sock and raised my voice,
raised it to the city, against the city, the city, the city,
then washed myself with vanilla sugar and rice.
Dripping wet, meatloaf made, framed pictures of the past—
the two of us on the cathedral steps, cupping
each other's faces. The clutter of a million collected
TV guides I thought meant something vanished
into the cloudless mid-day blue. I carved out
a place for us to live, kissed the hardwood
I shined myself, turned off the lights,
turned down the sheets, and slept.

BEFORE SAILING

Here in a new
manuscript lies the dress
  I unzipped on Sundays.
    The mindful post-coital conversations
  about going astray and

the prayer spoken
  sometime later
    in the silence of a separate room
  for these poems

to become realities.
  This one for example
    hides the scent of your return:
  lemon-pepper. I remember exactly

where I wasn't sitting
  when you opened the door,
    every note you didn't sing
  to quiet my anxious heart

back to sleep before
sailing silently away.

I Pause to Remember the Experience of Your Nose Piercing

You sitting on the surgeon's table, tight fisted,
me without the courage to close my eyes,
and a woman neither of us had previously met
clutching a long black nail,
ready to stake your nose.
It was often like this.
The two of us sitting slightly nervous
in a room not our own.
A third party ready to take one of us down.

Forgiving the Bastard who Keyed my Car

I must imagine his child waking up with a mouth
packed with cankers, her pale hair fallen
to her feet, her feet missing toes.
I must imagine her stomach
having recently lost its lining,
her widowed father crying himself awake
every twenty minutes or so.
I must imagine him in a torn apron—
what he uses for a winter coat—
running with blackened slippers through hail
to the doctor's office, collapsing from exhaustion,
the doctor running to catch him.
I must imagine the doctor as overweight and concerned,
demanding a warm cloth, steamed milk,
seeing the father's face, already knowing his story,
what must be done to save the little girl.
I must imagine the father protesting at first
when he reads the prescription,
and then, seeing the doctor nodding slowly,
nodding slowly himself.
I must imagine the brittle unforgiving night
with him in it, scraping the left side
of my red 95 Chevy Blazer,
following doctor's orders,
obtaining the precious General Motors metal,
the needed iron, catching it in a wooden bowl, weeping—
I can't forgive if he is not weeping—
and I must imagine the sick girl
in a second story window,

a frail hairless liver-spotted arm
outstretched in his direction,
yelling as loud as one can yell
with one vocal cord,
Don't do it Father! I'd rather die,
I'd rather die.

REASONS FOR WEEPING

Not because your death
carried with it another
bleeding heart.
Not because I loved you.
But because I felt so small
and so alone. One less person
to answer when I called.
One less person
who knew who I was.

For my First Wife, While Married to my Second

It has been a long time since we sat down
to green bean casserole. I hope Richard
has recovered. Emily and I have finally settled
meaning I'm tired now and safe
but mostly, in trouble. It's not that I wish
differently. It's not that I miss the money.
It's just that—the children have started
their sledding, the snow has gotten them out
of the house and yesterday, I spotted you
at the supermarket touching the nectarines,
looking like you couldn't put your mind
on something you needed. If we never speak again,
that would be fine—honestly, I have nothing to say.
But maybe you do. And maybe I could sit with my arms
unfolded, kind-of closing my eyes. I mean,
I'd like to hear you without hearing myself.
I mean, if you needed butter to borrow,
if you came up short, maybe, I would have it.
That's all, that's all I want to say.

HOW WE PRAYED

for James Tripp

How we prayed for a kind God, despite our knowing,
    our pasty shoulders Igored respectively,
    our little hairy arms outstretched in cliché.
And how we imagined Him reciting Milton, singing him
atop the windowsills in one instant,
sweeping banana peels below us in the next,
His heroed heart half pumping with apology.
How we expected Him to greet every last one
    with an uncallused hand and two beach-blanket eyes,
how we delighted in an empty hell
and imagined together, a saturated inn, bruised with healing
and how surprised we were when the mat below us read
    Welcome
    in someone else's blood,
and how, before we stepped through the door,
He offered to massage our screaming feet.

SHE ASKS IF WE CAN STILL BE FRIENDS

A woman, alone, rows a boat.
She is nothing
save muscle and wood.

Is thirsty. Has spent the last
year rowing.
Has only what she needs

to survive: seven mangoes,
exceptional intelligence,
unusual courage, fear.

She craves sand and shade.
Needs meat
and sleep. She sees something

in the distance, is it, yes,
an island.
She wants on. Steps

out of the boat exhausted.
There is a house.
There is a door. He sits

at a desk, alone. His back
to her. He may
be wearing a fedora, sandals.

Anyway, he is bearded. He turns.
She sits. He stands.
The door is still open.

It is a beautiful day.
He sees a boat.
He takes only what he needs

to survive.

CHAPTER ONE

BEGINNING

I have known no stillness
like this, blanketing the blackbird
at my feet, huge as someone else's life.
You could touch it
if you wanted. And I do.
Someone has to close its eyes.
Any moment, I think,
it could break into one
of a thousand lives.
Strong capable flight.
Thick gorgeous flight.
It's six o clock in the morning.
I'm alone, having recently tripped
over love and broken my body.
I have nothing to offer. It is over.
Death can be beautiful
on a bird that size.
This cruel magnificent morning—
the sky is so bright
people everywhere
are opening their windows.

Upon Hearing that She and the Man with whom She Cheated are Getting Married

after Mary Oliver

Somewhere behind me
the staccato of young men,
their laughter, a fitting truth,
something I wish I had
moments ago when the news
covered my body like sudden
rain. Beside me, an umbrella
I've carried since early morning—
I hope to God I don't forget it
when it's time again to leave.
I've ruined more evenings that way,
my shoes soaked, my body shaking.
I don't know what kind of animal
love is. I do know how to pray
on bent knees for someone
else's failure. From the ledge
of a lonely and startled dream,
I put my hands together and begin
the way anyone would: Dear God.

Epithalamion for 25 Years Come January

for Bill and Jean

Some pages, capable of saving your life,
you will never read. Not once in rain,
not ever in a car to your mother's.

Some words, for as long as you shall speak
and breathe, you will never utter.
And some thoughts, classics I know,

within your reach, you will never think,
neither in prayer nor profit, reason nor regret.
That's simply the way of it.

Certain books, however, yellowed
from touching, the binding held together
by duct tape and glue, you pick up night after

night, before falling asleep. And day after
day, you still wonder who MacArthur is,
why he appears without warning in Chapter 7

with a love letter. This doesn't stop you
from cheering, then falling asleep before
he hands it to sweet Delilah. Every night

your commitment to love begins by putting on pajamas
and lying down. Even after all these years,
you love putting on pajamas and lying down,

opening the book, reading the dedication,
cheering for the letter, the stunning question mark
of its delivery, the long committed dot dot dot.

OVER OUR MUFFINS

I'll pretend I'm on the brink of it,
and I'll wave my wintry hands
back and forth over the breakfast table,
your face will open with a laugh,
and we will speak over the muffins
of our former brilliance
before we are snared by the day:
I in a forgetful suit, my breath in the air,
and you down on your only knees,
asking for the rest of my life.
Our beautiful barking bodies
demanding most everything,
and everything, that restless instigator,
smirking at our latest craziness.

How did we marry?
I barely knew your mother,
and you who knew we were building better seasons,
you were just learning to kiss my mouth
as I was learning to use it.
Who could imagine me, a lifetime later,
sitting and looking into the museum of your eyes,
a piece of bran dangling from my bottom lip,
passing you the orange juice,
and you, humming through a napkin, rising from your seat?
Who could have predicted the miracle of you
dressing for the workday
and the wonder of me, before waking the little sleeper,
beginning to wash the morning things?

INSTRUCTIONS TO A LIFELONG FRIEND

Relax. You watered the chrysanthemums.
You turned the oven off. Breathe. Breathe again.
Spend more than you should for tea. Use what's left
to buy a postcard. Mail to Christopher
Goodrich. Let him know you are still standing.
Still a witness to beauty. Waking up
at 7am and leaving traces. Your mother
would like two poached eggs and an orange slice.
And your father, he loved you.
He did not die without telling you so. Feel your feet.
Your powerful arms. Well-appointed aren't they?
Breathe. Relax. Eat a salad. Use cucumbers
this time. You are made of hard work.
And good work. Concentrate on those you need.
Take them to a movie. Love again.
And prove that you can again and again.
Don't move so much. You turned the oven off.
The chrysanthemums, watered. Relax.
The moon is rising—it could be different.
You don't smoke. Isn't that something?
You live so simply. Driven by the most
acute affection. You should hit something.
And read Beckett and pay rent for four years.
Buy that girl a dress. Then take it off her.
Love her too much, while you have the opportunity.
Kiss something. Kiss something.
If the reason you wake is to give
and take, please kiss something.

A Thing Like Weather

Once again I return to happiness,
which means something, somewhere is in bloom

and the notion, however ridiculous,
is born again: love will not go on without me.

See how a thing like weather changes
everything? The warm earth spins a little at a time

so I won't lose my footing, and the April wind
pushes me toward collecting what it is I came for:

the belief that even in the beautiful places,
I am exceptionally possible.

FIDELITY

for James Dickey, after James Dickey's ADULTERY

We have both lived a little too long
In rooms a little too small for our furniture.
Often we are standing arms folded, empty hearted,

In doorways   one of us clutching a candlestick
One of us bleeding from the nose   gazing far
Far away   through the eyes of our parents

Now long dead   one of us may be fixing
A pot-roast   one of us shivering
From rain. This is the language of thirty

Years. There is usually a pitchfork
Between us   and someone is sometimes howling
Moonwards   so as not to die from too much death.

How can we say nothing can come
Of this   when so much already has:
You know what time I wake to piss

And I have swallowed your cheap California charm
At many a forgotten dinner party. We come together
And we go together, and if one of us

Is late or sad, the other is inches away,
Looking for leftovers. But we would not give
It up, for we are bettered

By bitching by braying even a little
Disaster   is reason for staying.
One could always leave

Always leave   always leave
The television on. And we have both tasted
That torture my love.

But I have known no beauty
Like the one of return. And I will forever whisper your
Name to the darkness. And you will forever wonder

Why I'm laughing we,
Who have had the courage to stay,
God blessed us. Some magic must be earned.

supine on a Serta, and assuming you are sitting next to me,
your head resting on my chest, your hand
reaching for your forehead, I ask
that you force my eyelids open
and position my eyebrows two or so inches
above their normal setting and urge my mouth,
if you don't mind, from its parched post
into the shape of an O,
three fingers long, two fingers wide.

That way, once you are through grieving
and have alerted the children,
it will appear as if I'm on the verge of song,
a rendition of "Walking my Baby Back Home,"—
not the traditional 1952 sing-a-long,
more like James Taylor's fevered acoustic cry
to a woman since departed.

And if you would then move my left leg
so it's nearly touching the floor,
and budge the right with bended knee,
so it might easily follow the left,
I could fool you into believing I am rising
for one final embrace, and who knows,
we might dance a two step
up the skinny hall and down again,
my lips fixed to sing the song whose steady rise and fall
will keep the rhythm as we sway left to right, right to left.

THE MARRIAGE BED

One of us is the one who takes
everything for granted. The other
responsible for the long discussion

on who we become in the off hours,
what distances have led us away
from the marriage bed.

This is what it means
to need too much, then,
not enough. The mattress

hasn't been rotated in months,
should be replaced. It means
the bedroom window I stare out of

on these occasions, pretending
you are not behind me,
reflects the woman you are,

finally, as you lay your body down
in truce, your silence a meeting place,
a heartache, a long letting go

and then, ahhhh, a grabbing hold again.

COUNTING SHEEP

A little spiral moon, a pasture,
well groomed, and they're off—
each with his number dutifully

attached to wool by thick string.
The first is, perhaps, too eager. His ability
disturbs me. The second feels more authentic,

a lazy gallop through worn daisies before
clearing the fence. The third has my father's
bearded mouth and the fourth is my father,

slowly shaking his head. The fifth is you,
my love, in April. Six, the absence of you.
Seven, April in Paris,

two lovers skinny dipping the Seine. Eight
is their midnight quarrel, someone
has forgotten the towels. Nine,

the towels themselves, hidden all this time
by ten, who, thankfully, is a sheep again. Eleven
tells twelve the bent fence is imaginary

and twelve refuses to jump. It's hard
not to kill him, but I reason him over,
remind him what must be done. Thirteen,

because it's late, carries fourteen, and fifteen,
a newborn, scrapes a hoof before reaching
the hurdle. I lift him, put him to bed,

and take his place. The earth is a ripe
damp beneath my feet. The air, so soft
mid-jump, it's likely I'll do this all night—

THE BACK SEAT

The first time in years
I held my hand to my heart

was after you said *Listen,*
the beat's abnormal.

Before long we were kissing
though who began it I don't remember.

In the end, even that doesn't matter.
We were young. We were kissing.

FORGIVENESS

At the end
of this frozen ground,
this sharpened day,
these bleeding fingertips,

at the end of two roads, then another,
the end of my clenched
and bleating body,
the end of my father, then my mother,

I rest my feet,
lift my chin to mercy.
And lift. And lift.

ACKNOWLEDGMENTS

Grateful acknowledgements are made to the journals in which some of these poems first appeared:

5AM: "For my First Wife, While Married to my Second"
Cider Press Review: "Epithalamion for 25 Years Come January"
Cimarron Review: "Spotless"
Comrades Journal: "Because It's Important"
Entelechy International: "I Pause to Remember the Experience of Your Nose Piercing," "If I Didn't Open My Arms," "Tooth Fairy Dies"
Hotel Amerika: "Assuming I Die with My Eyes Closed"
Inkblots: "Over Our Muffins"
Karamu: "Icarus Explains"
Kestrel: "Beginning," "Forgiving the Bastard who Keyed my Car," "Going to Bed Angry"
The Kit Cat Review: "Art of Leaving," "Instructions to a Life Long Friend"
Main Street Rag: "Our Elephant"
The New York Quarterly: "To the Woman Whose Nose Ran into Our Frisbee, July 13 2003, Ft. Green Park, and To the Blood That Would Not Stop Gushing," "You, Me, My Mom, My Dad"
Rattle: "Say it with a Mix-Tape"
The Sycamore Review: "Counting Sheep"
The Worcester Review: "By Reaching," "A Thing Like Weather" won a Dorothy Sargent Rosenberg Poetry Prize.
"For my First Wife, While Married to my Second" was featured on *Verse Daily*.

Huge, love-strewn thanks to Paula for her vigilant watch over these poems. Thanks also to Alicia, Gerry and Anne Marie and dear beautiful Rachel.

CHRISTOPHER GOODRICH currently teaches in Montgomery County, Maryland. He has also taught for Frostburg University and New York University. His poems have appeared in the *Worcester Review*, *Rattle*, *Hotel Amerika*, *Cimarron Review*, *Margie*, *Sycamore Review*, *Natural Bridge*, *The New York Quarterly*, *5am*, and *Verse Daily* among others. He is the recipient of a Dorothy Sargent Rosenberg Poetry Prize and holds an MFA from New England College. This is his first full-length collection. He lives with a five-year-old terrier named Seamus and his wife Rachel, who will soon deliver their first child.